Bridget

Kate

Santa

Storysongs to readalong

Kahuna Kidsongs

FourTunes

Vince

Mr Bling

Ishbel

Jim

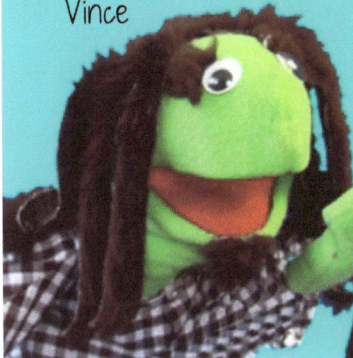

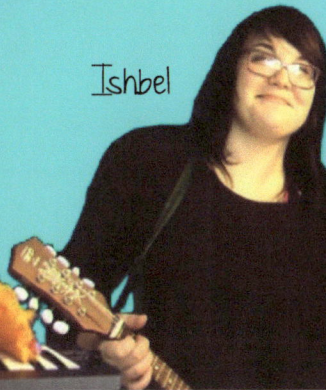

FourTunes

Storysongs to readalong

Welcome to Kahuna Kidsongs FourTunes, a whirlwind tour through whimsical lands with crazy characters, improbable plots, catchy tunes, sing-along songs and maybe a little learning on the way…

Contents

ISBN978-0-9951004-0-4

All songs and stories written and produced by Jim Cullinane.

Thanks to Ishbel Cullinane for her super singing.

KahunaKidsongs.com

Kahuna Kidsongs

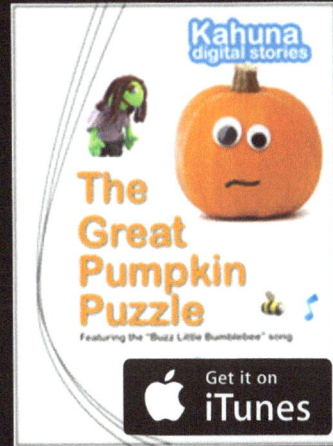

The Great Pumpkin Puzzle

Kahuna digital stories

Featuring the "Buzz Little Bumblebee" song

Get it on iTunes

Little Bumblebee

Feat. Vince
the Vegetarian
Veggie Grower

Busy bumblebee buzzing 'round.
I like your bumblebee sound.

You're fun to have around, when you buzz,
buzz, buzz, little bumblebee. (x2)

You're a happy, hairy, little bumbling bee.
Buzzing about you're a bit clumsy.

Bouncing off the flowers and leaves
when you
buzz, buzz, buzz, little bumblebee. (x2)

You're tougher than the honey bees,
you'll take off at just 6 degrees.

A little shiver to warm your wings
then you
buzz, buzz, buzz, little bumblebee. (x2)

Lots of birds chirp and tweet
and while their sound is pretty sweet,

the garden sound I really love,
is that low down bumblebee buzz
– little bumblebee.

You're a happy, humble, little bumblebee.
Furry, fuzzy, funny
mustn't grumble bee.

You're the bee I like to see you
buzz, buzz, buzz little bumblebee. (x2)

C'mon and
buzz, buzz, buzz little bumblebee!

C'mon and
buzz, buzz, buzz little bumblebee!

C'mon and…
(take a big breath!)

Buzzzzzzzzzzzzzz!

Kahuna Kidsongs

MR BLING

HE'S THE KING OF THE
LATEST THING

Mr Bling is… blingy, blingy.

Mr Bling is… blingy, blingy.

Mr Bling is… blingy, blingy.
Ding, Ding, Mr Bling!

Mr Bling's got blingy clothes.
They sparkle wherever he goes.

Blingy fingers and blingy toes.
Everybody knows…

Mr Bling is… blingy, blingy.
Mr Bling is… blingy, blingy.

Mr Bling is… blingy, blingy.
Ding, Ding, Mr Bling!

Mr Bling, when he goes outside,
he's got a blingy car for a ride.

It's blingy long and it's blingy wide.
It's his source of pride.

Mr Bling is… blingy, blingy.
Mr Bling is… blingy, blingy.

Mr Bling is… blingy, blingy.
Ding, Ding, Mr Bling!

When he's alone at night,
Mr Bling don't feel so bright.

Seems he's got everything,
but there's some things
money just can't bring.

Poor Mr Bling is… blingy, blingy.
Mr Bling is… blingy, blingy.

Mr Bling is… blingy, blingy.
Ding, Ding, Mr Bling!

Mr Bling's got blingy shoes,
a blingy hat and a blingy do.

A blingy bed and a blingy loo
he does blingy number twos!

Mr Bling is… blingy, blingy.
Mr Bling is… blingy, blingy.

Mr Bling is… blingy, blingy.
Ding, Ding, Mr Bling!

Mr Bling's like you and me,
he wants to buy everything he sees.

A new iPad or a new TV,
but he can't afford it, unfortunately!

Mr Bling is… blingy, blingy.
Mr Bling is… blingy, blingy.

Mr Bling is… blingy, blingy.
Ding, Ding, Mr Bling!

When he's alone at night,
Mr Bling don't feel so bright.

Sure he's got all the bling
but don't miss the important things
Mr Bling, bling, bling, bling.

Mr Bling is… blingy, blingy.

Mr Bling is… blingy, blingy.

Mr Bling is… blingy, blingy.

Ding, Ding, Mr Bling! (x4)

Ding ding!

SANTA'S HAT

Kahuna Kidsongs

Reindeer waiting by the sleigh
getting ready for Christmas day.

To spread some joy
throughout the world
especially for the boys and girls.

But wait a minute, where is he?
Santa's not where he's supposed to be.

It's time they all got on their way
because tomorrow is Christmas day.

But Santa Claus is running late
and so the reindeer must wait.

He can't find his Santa hat,
now I wonder where that hat is at?

He's in a fluster, running around,
wishing that his hat be found.

It covers up his baldy patch
so Santa needs his Santa hat!

The elves are helping in the search
they've checked the workshop
and the church.

Where - oh - where can his hat be?
Have they checked
under the Christmas tree?

'Cause Santa Claus is running late
and so the reindeer must wait.

He can't find his Santa hat
I wonder where that hat is at?

It looks like Christmas might be late
or be postponed to a later date.

Who would have thought
that Santa's hat
could cause something as BIG as that!

One elf wisely checks the loo
'cause Santa goes, and so do you.

And hanging on the bathroom door
is the hat that they've been looking for!

So Santa Claus puts on his hat
and the sleigh is gone in 5 seconds flat.

He's got a lot of catching up to do
I hope he comes and visits you.

Merry Christmas, merry Christmas,
merry Christmas, to you.

Merry Christmas, merry Christmas,
merry Christmas, to you.

Merry Christmas, merry Christmas,
merry Christmas, to you.

Ho, ho, ho, Merry Christmas everybody
and a happy New Year!

Kahuna Kidsongs

Someday

Some day I'm gonna rise above,
spread my wings and take off, someday.

Get away from this old town,
this place only holds me down, someday.

'Cause I know I can do it if I try.

Because someday, someday I'm gonna fly.

Someday I'm gonna be long gone.

These wings aren't just painted on, someday.

Pack my bags and say goodbye,

'cause this little kiwi's born to fly, someday.

'Cause I know I can do it if I try.

Because someday, someday I'm gonna fly.

Someday, someday soon,
I'm gonna fly, fly around the moon.

And everyone,
everyone will know my name,
and things will never, ever be the same.

Someday I'll be overseas.

Take off on my big O.E. - someday.

There's no reason I should stay.

That's why I've gotta get away - someday.

'Cause I know I can do it if I try.

Because someday,

someday I'm gonna fly

'Cause I know I can do it if I try.

Because someday,

someday I'm gonna fly - someday…

43

Kahuna Kidsongs

storysongs to read along

Digital DIY

Way before humans could write, we told our stories through songs and poems. The rhythmn, rhyme and repetition of language involves the audience, making it memorable. What's more, these elements are proven to help children learn reading too, so we thought, why just say it when you can sing it?

Based at Windybot Farm in North Canterbury, New Zealand, Jim Cullinane is a former teacher and Digital DIYer who uses old toys, handmade puppets, ukuleles and iPads to create homespun, cheeky and cheerful stories, songs, videos and interactive eBooks to help engage children in reading.

He also runs iPad Labs in schools and libraries to get kids interested in making their own digital stories, songs, movies, and eBooks too.

Please visit our website to check out our other songs, stories and videos, from horsing around with Horsey Horse to brave bumblebees, prancing pirates, groovy gumboots, monsters, Mothers day and a whole lot more…

KahunaKidsongs.com